NATIONAL
GEOGRAPHIC

This Is an Island

Belle Perez

This is an island.
There is water
all around the island.

There is a **waterfall** on the island.

There is a **mountain**
on the island.

There is a **forest** on the island.

There is a **beach** on the island.
There is water
all around the island.

Picture Glossary

 beach  mountain

 forest  waterfall

 island

12